TIM CRESSWELL

Tim Cresswell is a geographer and poet. He is the author or editor of over a dozen books on the themes of place and mobility. His most recent title is *Maxwell Street: Writing and Thinking Place* (University of Chicago Press, 2019). His poems are widely published on both sides of the Atlantic, including in *The Rialto*, *Poetry Wales*, *Magma*, *The Moth*, *LemonHound* and *Salamander*. He has published three collections of poetry: *Soil* (2013), *Fence* (2015) and *Plastiglomerate* (2020). He co-edits the interdisciplinary journal *GeoHumanities* and is the first Visiting Professor at the Centre for Place Writing at Manchester Metropolitan University. Tim lives and works in Edinburgh where he is Ogilvie Professor of Geography at the University of Edinburgh.

ALSO BY TIM CRESSWELL

POETRY

Plastiglomerate (Penned in the Margins, 2020)
Soil (Penned in the Margins, 2013)

CRITICAL WORKS

Maxwell Street: Writing and Thinking Place (University of Chicago, 2019)
Place: An Introduction (Blackwell, 2014)
Geographic Thought: A Critical Introduction (Blackwell, 2013)
On the Move: Mobility in the Modern Western World (Routledge, 2006)
The Tramp in America (Reaktion, 2001)
In Place/Out of Place: Geography, Ideology and Transgression (University of Minnesota, 1996)

Fence

Tim Cresswell

Penned in the Margins
LONDON

PUBLISHED BY PENNED IN THE MARGINS
Toynbee Studios, 28 Commercial Street, London E1 6AB
www.pennedinthemargins.co.uk

All rights reserved
© Tim Cresswell 2020

The right of Tim Cresswell to be identified as the author of this work has been asserted by him in accordance with Section 77 of the Copyright, Designs and Patent Act 1988.

This book is in copyright. Subject to statutory exception and to provisions of relevant collective licensing agreements, no reproduction of any part may take place without the written permission of Penned in the Margins.

First published 2015

This edition published 2020

Printed in the United Kingdom by CPI Group (UK) Ltd

ISBN
978-1-908058-31-7

This book is sold subject to the condition that it shall not, by way of trade or otherwise, be lent, re-sold, hired out, or otherwise circulated without the publisher's prior consent in any form of binding or cover other than that in which it is published and without a similar condition including this condition being imposed on the subsequent purchaser.

ACKNOWLEDGEMENTS

This book would not exist without an invitation from the artist Alex Hartley and his producer Claire Doherty to join them and a maverick crew on the good ship Noorderlicht on a two-week adventure in Svalbard and the ongoing endeavours of the nowhereisland project. It remains one of the highlights of my life.

Fence started as a modest sequence until various people along the way encouraged me to develop it into the form it now takes. Foremost among these is Srikanth (Chicu) Reddy who acted as a thoughtful and encouraging critical voice during my month as part of the Writing Studio at the Banff Center in Alberta, Canada in May 2014. I also benefitted tremendously from the dedicated guidance of Karen Solie and Suzanne Buffam while at Banff. I am grateful to all the other participants in the Writing Studio but particularly Dick Capling for the Martinis.

I will always be indebted to the ongoing mentorship and friendship of Jo Shapcott. The year spent with Jo and Andrew Motion developing and teaching a Masters course on *Place, Environment, Writing* at Royal Holloway clearly found its way into the words on the pages that follow. Anja Konig and Sarah de Leeuw read and helpfully commented on parts of this along the way. Audiences for readings at the Writers Read series in

Montreal, at Cornell University in Ithaca, New York and Queens University, Kingston, Ontario provided useful feedback. I remain ever grateful to Tom Chivers for his faith in my work and for his endless energy in promoting innovative poetry.

Finally I am indebted most of all to my wife Carol and wonderful creative children, Owen, Sam and Maddy.

The North is one vast, massive, glorious corruption of rock and language

LORINE NIEDECKER, 'LAKE SUPERIOR'

Fence

i

Post

Post

Post

Post

Post

Post

Post

ii

we stand semi-circled   staring
at rust red metal poles   spaced
in regular   intervals
along an Arctic beach
hip-height   unconnected
separating us   from
the nothing-in-particular   beyond
strewn rocks
            scattered
        haphazard
grey red black boulders in a shallow rise
80 degrees north
like Franz Joseph Land   Nunavut
protecting what   from us
or us   from

iii

Spitzbergen   north
further   than the Samoieds
than Siberia   Nova Sembla
the agitated sea   bristling
mountains   cracked   split
waves spit fury   against granite capes
islands of ice broke   open
echoes of   musket shot reports
wind-raised snow columns   hoarse moanings
a choir from   the old world
ushers in   the new

July 31st 1838

iv

    we arrived at the northernmost airport
        with year round scheduled flights
    strolled the northernmost settlement
      with over a thousand souls
  home of the northernmost blues festival
  passed the northernmost church
took cash from the northernmost ATM
sent postcards from the northernmost post office
    ate from the northernmost kebab van run by an
      asylum seeker from Iran
in rolling seas
eighty degrees north
    we held the northernmost disco
on the *Noorderlicht*
dancing to Talking Heads

    now the northernmost fence

v

how did I get here
two flights   touched

down in Tromsø   a red boat
fore cabin   fell

over   and over
seasick   travelworn

frayed   at the edges
almost   not moving

eighty degrees   north
no land   nor stars

I travelled
to the ends of the

vi

my dear brother
like everyone   you wonder
how I undertake
this great project when you
see me start with such fear

the interest in my story will grow
as I reach the high latitudes of
Old Europe   my arrival will benefit
from the merit of originality
being the only woman who
has undertaken such a journey

here's our route

Holland   Hamburg   Denmark   Sweden
Western Norway   Christiania   Trondheim
the North Cape and   finally   Spitzbergen

if it please God

June (?) 1838

vii

Amsterdam is still a gay city
lively and picturesque
everything interesting for the traveller

Brouk is not a city or a village
more an agglomeration of houses
crafted by owners
rich enough to follow their addictions

Hamburg is delightfully located between
the sea and hills covered with fertile plains
at the bottom of the hills   the Elbe turns
like a big snake in tall grass

Copenhagen is one of the richest   most learned   cities
it contains valuable collections of
medals   bas-reliefs   Etruscan vases
a natural history museum famous for its beautiful shells

Dronthehn or   if you like   Trondheim

as locals and geographers call it
is a wood city which burns every ten
years   the people do not care

one day in Tromsø
is much longer
than is necessary
to know the place by heart
being eager to leave
I re-embarked

Hammerfest   these ten letters
do not do you justice
the northernmost city that exists
the last cluster of houses
in this strange corner of the world

May-July 1838

viii

starts marked by accidents   small conspiracies
hidden geniuses   oppose my wanderlust

crossing Paris   a poorly harnessed horse
leaving Le Havre   a violent sea smashing wooden wheels
Amsterdam   grounded on a sandbar
Trondheim   thick fog   forcing us to anchor

leaving Hammerfest   tacking
too close to land   we nearly break our bowsprit
high waves   force return to port   to repair
at last we head out to the full
Arctic Ocean   with returning happy hearts

July 17th 1838

ix

two weeks out of range   no signal
    iPhones off
clad in neoprene   merino wool
    hi-performance fleece   breathable shells
we roll off zodiacs like marines   dive-bombed by a skua
    alert to our trespasses

our guide stands guard with his banger
    flares and rifle   keeping polar bears at bay

red rock backdrop   to yellow sweep
    of sand   the moss
brilliant green   fragile   off limits
    an eroded path to   glacier blue

a cabin stands empty   home for two guards in high season
    keeping tourists off tombs

x

Driftwood — whalebones — walrus teeth — unicorn horns rather of some sea creature than any land beast — these things the sea casts forth upon the barrens

July 1613

xi

William Barents called
this Tusk Bay   Robert
Fotherby   claiming the
fjord for England
called it Maudlen Sound
and this spot   Trinity
Harbor   the Dutch came
with another name
Magdalenen Sond
and then   Maria Magdalene
Sond   now the fjord is
Norwegian   it's
Magdalenefjorden
and this spot   Gravneset
which means 'grave site'

xii

I went to the harbour — caused a cross to be set up — the kings arms nailed there — the Muscovy Company's mark — the day of the month and year of our Lord

cutting up a piece of earth — which afterward I carried aboard our ship — I took it in my hand and said

I take this piece of earth, as a sign of lawful possession of this country of King James his New-Land, and of this particular place, which I name Trinity Harbour, taken on behalf of the company of merchants called the Merchants of New Trades and Discoveries, for the use of our Sovereign Lord James, by the grace of God King of Great Brittaine, France, and Ireland, whose royal arms are here set up, to the end that all people who shall here arrive may take notice of his Majesties right and title to this country, and to every part thereof. God save King James.

22nd *June 1614*

xiii

as if giants gave up
playing pick-up-sticks
leaving lumber
    scattered
over silt and sand
sun-silvered larch   spruce   fir
    carried from Siberia
    by currents and the fall of
    Communism
bits of old dock
escapees from sawmills
    wash up
    where blue ice
    groans and cracks
before the two inch willows

xiv

Robert Fotherby
Englishman   explorer   whaler
staked his claim in the name
of King James I
right here
with a wooden cross and
the King's arms

    'Twas sixteen hundred and fourteen
    There she blows boys! There she blows!
    When Fotherby blew in on the Thomasine
    There she blows boys! There she blows!

Fotherby of the Muscovy
Company — granted
a monopoly on whaling

    There she blows boys! There she blows!
    His boat is crowding on full sail
    There she blows boys! There she blows!

Seeking out the Greenland whale

this was territory
for the industry
this spot
a station for whalers

He's coming here to stake his claim
There she blows boys! There she blows!
In the name of good King James
There she blows boys! There she blows!

xv

Trinity Harbor.
Maudlin Sound.
Wiches Sound.
Red Cliff Sound.
Red Beach.
Redbeach Point.
Castlin's Point.
Point Welcome.
Sir Thomas Smith's Inlet.
Point Deceit.

xvi

                      the lowest fence is the easiest to get across
love your neighbour but keep your fence
                    good fences make good neigbours
          sitting on the fence
             silence is a fence around wisdom
   when you see a turtle on a fence post
you know he had some help
don't tell your secret
          not even to a fence
               a fence between
makes love more keen
       a garden without a fence
is like a dog without a tail
             the only fence against the world
is a thorough knowledge of it
our civilization is essentially one of property
              of fences

xvii

from the middle English *fens*
from the Old French *defense*
from the Latin *defendere*
to protect or defend
as in *defence*

in the 14th century *fence*
meant the act of defending
in the 15th century *fence*
became a thing

a barrier
or enclosure
this fence

by the 17th century *fence*
meant to use a sword in combat
and a dealer in stolen goods

the Norwegian for *fence* is *gjerde*

meaning farm   estate   land   courtyard
from the Old Norse *garðr*
from the Proto-Germanic *gardaz*
meaning to enclose
as in *yard*
or *garden*

related to the Old Saxon *gard*
yard   garden   court   region   land
dwelling

xviii

strike near the swimming fin — low under the water — to pierce into his entrails — when wounded — he can wrest the lance from the striker's hand — sometimes two men are needed to pluck it out — but one did thrust it in — he will frisk and strike with his tail — very forcibly — sometimes hitting the shallop — splitting her asunder — sometimes maiming — or killing — men

1614

xviv

sitting quietly on deck   nestled
under fur   I heard my name muttered
from amongst a group of sailors

*whose idea was it to bring this woman
with us?*   *a pale woman*   *petite
with feet like ladyfingers
hands that never raised an oar*   *as chilly
as a Senegal parakeet in Paris.
Assuming the ice takes us*   *she will
be first to die*

    there was silence as they
revived their pipes

if the ice closed in   my death was certain
despite kindness   the floor lined
with reindeer skins   tightly closed windows
the down-filled quilt   more a nest
than a room

          despite these excellent precautions
I suffered from the cold   was forced to exercise
at night   for warmth

July 1838

xx

blueing hands   tearing eyes
I am travelled   lost

compass gone   haywire
so north

spinning   unable to read
traces   tracks in the moss

along the shore
polar bear prints

scat from a meagre meal
skeleton hand

of a seal
this fence   these rocks

xxi

we skirted Prince Charles Island —
a long slice of loose dirt —
dropped anchor in a small deep bay
called Magdalena Bay
on English maps

we had reached the goal of our adventure
Spitsbergen!

July 31st 1838

xxii

Gravneset (Grave headland) is surrounded by majestic mountains. Located on the northwest coast of the island of Spitsbergen, Norway, Magdalenafjord sits about 750 miles from the frosty North Pole. Tall glaciers and magnificent nature in one of the most beautiful fjords in Svalbard. Its crystal-clear waters reflect the ebony shades of the rugged snow-peaked mountains nearby, which stand in stark contrast to the blue-tinged glacier skimming off into the sea. Through the course of Svalbard's history, few places have been as frequently visited as Gravneset; it remains one of the most popular sites of cultural heritage. Fortunately, the majesty of the fjord's dramatic scenery was undisturbed and it remains a haven for wildlife.

xxiii

~~Gravneset (Grave headland)~~ is **surrounded by** ~~majestic mountains. Located on the northwest coast of the island of Spitsbergen, Norway, Magdalenafjord sits about 750 miles from the frosty North Pole. Tall glaciers and magnificent nature in one of the most beautiful fjords in Svalbard. Its crystal-clear waters reflect the ebony shades of the rugged snow-peaked mountains nearby, which stand in~~ **stark contrast** ~~to the blue-tinged glacier skimming off into the sea. Through the course of Svalbard's history,~~ **few places have been as frequently** ~~visited as Gravneset; it remains one of the most popular sites of cultural heritage. Fortunately, the majesty of the fjord's dramatic scenery was un~~**disturbed** ~~and it remains a haven for wildlife.~~

xxiv

                        nearby   stand   stark

remains

XXV

motionless   loneliness
follows lively antics   a flotilla of icebergs
surrounds the corvette   architecture
everywhere   needles become
mushrooms   a column copies
a huge table   a tower mimics
a staircase   bell towers   minarets
arches   pyramids
turrets   domes
niches   scrolls
arcades   pediments
sitting colossus   delicate sculptures
like those   on cathedral pillars

July 30th 1838

xxvi

when I was far from home   when
I was north   when
I had grown accustomed   to blue ice
and the absence
of trees   I stumbled in
with my clamorous crowd
cameras and calamity
our sudden smells
reds and greens   guide books
gizmos and gadgetry   our clickety-clack
filling   the wind
like we had misplaced
the space around us and thought
we might find it

xxvii

upon the land, there be many
white bears
    grey foxes
    a great many deer
    also white pheasant
    wild geese
    sea pigeons
    sea parrots
willock, stint and gulls

and some unworthy of naming

1613

xxviii

these rocks mark graves of whalers
and these are blubber ovens
to render whale oil

the Dutch called whale oil
   train oil
from the Dutch word *traan*
meaning *tear*
   or *drop*

xxix

soil   bone-covered
walrus bones   seal bones
great fish-bones
time whitened   ice preserved
whole skeletons
fleshless seal fingers   like human hands
inhabitants   of a foundered city

I left this charnel-house
found myself in a cemetery
a foundered city
relics upon   the snow
coffins   half open
empty   of bodies
gnawed by bear teeth

the sturdy arms of 'the fat man in a furred robe'
had displaced the stones   devastated
the tombs   several bones
scattered   half-broken   gnawed

sad remains   of a foundered city

31ˢᵗ July 1838

xxx

Desirous   while recognising the sovereignty of Norway over the Archipelago of Spitsbergen   including Bear Island   of seeing these territories provided with an equitable regime   in order to assure their development and peaceful utilisation

High Contracting Parties   recognise

    West Spitsbergen
    North-East Land
    Barents Island
    Edge Island
    Wiche Islands
    Hope Island or Hopen-Eiland
    Prince Charles Foreland
    all islands great or small
    rocks appertaining thereto

Ships and nationals   enjoy
        territories   and   their territorial waters

Norway shall be free
			of said regions and their territorial waters
it being clearly understood
			equally without privilege or favour
Occupiers of land   enjoy   hunting
			Nationals shall have equal
liberty   access   entry
			waters fjords ports territories
both on land and in the territorial waters
			territories shall have purpose
territories   respect   traffic
			in nation
No charge or restriction shall be imposed on
			territories or occupation of land
the same force and
			right of ownership of property including
in the territories
			complete conformity
Expropriation   grounds   compensation
			territories specified
from the point of view   of the State
			devoted to the said territories
shall not exceed   the object in view

The value shall be fixed

Done at Paris   the ninth day of February   1920   in duplicate   one copy to be transmitted to the Government of His Majesty the King of Norway   and one deposited in the archives of the French Republic; authenticated copies will be transmitted to the other Signatory Powers.

xxxi

                        this is the arctic skua
                                sharp-tailed
                                white-flashed
                                  black-capped
transequatorial kleptoparasitic migrant
                                      also called
                                  parasitic jaeger
                                    parasitic skua
                descends on puffins   terns
                                      attacking in
                                            midair
                              stealing food from
beaks or forces them to drop their
                              catch   swooping
                                        to catch
                       it before it   hits water
here is where it nests – the same spot every year
                                       a still point
                                  in a moving life
                          up from South Africa
nine month vagabond – three month settler
                                            migrant
                                                thief

xxxii

other names for the *Bowhead* include
    Balaena mysticetus
    Arctic Right Whale
    Greenland Right Whale
they were the 'right' whales to kill
    swam slowly
    surfaced regularly
    floated when dead

unlike humpbacks or blue whales
they did not migrate south during the year
instead they tarried

xxxiii

Full Name: Magdalena Fjord
Primary Country Code: SV (Svalbard)
Region Font Code: 1 (Americas/Western Europe)
Unique Feature Identifier: -2463384
Unique Name Identifier: -3393177
Latitude in decimal degrees: 79.583333
Longitude in decimal degrees: 10.966667
Latitude in degrees, minutes, and seconds: 79° 35' 00" N
Longitude in degrees, minutes, and seconds: 10° 58' 00" E
Military Grid Reference System coordinates:
   33XVJ1865237897
Joint Operations Graphic reference: NT29-04
Feature Classification: H (Hydrographic type feature)
Feature Designation Code: FJD (fjord)
Populated Place Classification: No data
Name Type: V (Variant or alternate name)
A form of the full name that allows for alphabetical sorting of the file into gazetteer sequence:
   MAGDALENAFJORD
Full Name with QWERTY characters: Magdalena Fjord
Modify Date: 1994-01-14

xxxiv

terra nullius   no-man's land
like the high seas   with its motley crews

or the moon   no-one to displace
this time   just bears

foxes   bowheads
nothing to   connect

no trees   no echoes

xxxv

most bore no inscription

on one   a friendly hand had knifecut
a no-longer legible name
Dortretcht   Hollande   1783

another   also nameless
had come from Bremen
his death dated 1697

but two coffins placed in the hollow
of a rock were in excellent keeping
the bodies still fleshy   clothed
nothing written of who they were
or where they were from

for the first time
I thought of France
my family   my friends
the fine sky

as to the dead   strewn around
not scholars   enraptured with discovery
lured by the unknown   just forsaken fishermen
seeking subsistence   for families

Norwegian   Russian   Dutch
their history was the same for all

31st July 1838

xxxvi

I counted fifty-two tombs
without epitaphs
without monuments
unwreathed
without reminiscences
nor tears
without regrets
or prayers

most desolate cemetery
where forgetfulness twice enshrouds the dead
where a sigh
or a voice
or even a footfall
is ever heard

31st July 1838

xxxvii

I lingered by the graves
full of pity   moved
absorbed   dreaming   praying

sketched the small peninsula

returned to the ship
pointed out its   absence
on the maps

the Captain named the peninsular
Tombeaux (Grave site)

31ˢᵗ July 1838

xxxviii

the whale is a sea beast of a huge bigness

1614

xxxix

    these mountains move too   *Devonian*
        Red Sandstone   also called
    Old Red Sandstone   rich in
iron oxide and scattered fossils
    of primitive armoured fish formed
        from the erosion of the
            Caledonian Mountains
children of a continental fenderbender
    AvaloniaBalticaLaurentia
before ice and all the names for blue
layered azure   robin's egg   cerulean   lapis
long before Longyearbyen   Oslo   Paris   before
    even Pangea   before
        even names   shifted up from
            Morocco   which wasn't Morocco
                to meet us here
red rock in   blue-grey north
    four hundred million years of wandering

xl

this fence:

metal posts mark out empty intervals
post   space   post   space   post   space

borders   boundaries   beating the bounds
once a year: post   post   post   post

post   sand   rockshards   lichen   post   driftwood
splintered   post   sand   birdshit   post   post   post

chainlengths   poles   planks   beams   barbed wire   electric
rips and zaps   snagged clothes   snarls of wool on nails

prairies   partitioned   triangulated   drawn and quartered
divisions   places for neighbourly gossip   fences

flattened by gale force four   or   sprawling across deserts
keeping Bedouin at bay   marking out forty acres

beside the rail tracks   or prison camps: fences as poems
begging attention   getting in the way   forcing

diversions: post   post   post   post   repeatable
infinite: post   post   post   post   making the

dull blank wilderness legible   comparable   exchangeable
what else makes nothing into fields   gardens   vacant lots

post   post   post   post   post   the patch
where dad had me paint panels with thick black

creosote   fireproof   pungent summer smell
posts pushing apart   post pulling in: welcome/refusal

keeping in/out   stockades and balustrades
pickets   palisades   chain-link   split-rail

this fence:

xli

his head one third part of the whole quantity — his finnes (which we call whalebone in England) — wholly included within his spacious mouth — rooted in his upper jaw — his eyes not much bigger than those of an ox — his body round — with a broad spreading tail — which is of a tough solid substance — used for to make chopping-blocks — to chop the blubber on

1614

xlii

        made of keratin
like human hair   or fingernails
also called whalebone
a misnomer

        used by Bowheads
to filter krill   copepods   fish
even small birds   opening
its mouth   scooping
shoals and water   pressing
tongue   against upper jaw
sieving out the prey

        worked
to frame umbrellas
stiffen collars   manufacture corset stays

baleen (from the Latin
bālaena   which means
whale)

xliii

cut off his head — containing tongue and teeth — tow it to the shore till high tide — haul it up with crabs and capstowes — wait for low tide — cut out teeth with hatchets — four or six at once — lug further ashore — severed each one from each — scrape off the pith from the ends of the teeth — with such scraping irons as coopers use — rub in the sand to strip the grease — sort into bundles of fifty — bind up with cords — tie a stick on each of them — on which is written some number — and the company's mark — ready to be shipped

1614

xliv

to make a corset (a pair   of *bodies*)   first make
a *basis*   stiff   strong   breathable   (linen is
best)   to place bones between   you will
need ten yards of good baleen   of various
assorted thicknesses   and enough linen
for two layers   you join them   with
a basting stitch   then   mark the
boning channels   then
sew them from bust to
waistline
line with satin ribbon
slip the bones in the channels
a busk is a must   inserted down
the front   to flatten   the bust and torso
in the way men like

xlv

he had her down in London
    belly to floor   hands
    outstretched   pointed
    toes   his foot
    on the small of her back
he pulled the ribbons tighter
    on her *basque*
    her *stay*
    her *corset*
desiring a sixteen-inch waist
    ribs compressed   organs
    constricted   breath
breasts lifted   parted
    bound in baleen from
    the Bowhead's mouth
anatomy as topography
    contours moulded
    vistas like Capability Brown
    rippled ribs   painted nipples
    drumlins   valleys
    moraines   kettle holes

she was thinking Jonah   swallowed
    by the whale
    whalespouts and icebergs
woman becoming whale
    her ribs and baleen merging
    bursting out   submarine
    down amongst the tentacles
    and mermaids   skin scarred with jagged ice
    singing   big whalebreaths   enough
    for half an hour   diving deep
    she was Bowhead   impossible
    too-big mouth   glittering
    starbubbles streaming from her skin
    into the dark   among
    the angler fish and luminous
    shrimp   lights flashing
    as the whalebreath
    ran out   oxygen
    diminished

he lifted her   hands over her head
    placed the baleen busk between her breasts
    pushing them apart

this was his gift
etched in bone   a sketch
of a whaling ship   his heart
forever

xlvi

at first   all went well
walruses plentiful
seals simple to capture
oil made on the coast itself
great green ivory walrus teeth
so esteemed in Sweden

they talked of the cargo's value
the profits and pleasures
of return   then
an unexpected cold
setting a firm and motionless sea
around their ship
the way home closed for nine
perhaps ten months

in such a place

at first they kept to the ship
warming themselves

with bear's grease   fish-bones   oil
everything on board that could be
burned as provisions dwindled
privations grew
polar bear   blue fox   ptarmigan   seal
hunted with renewed zeal

then   a terrible day
after the death of one of their number
after fearful sufferings
they warmed themselves
by burning the ship   holes dug in the ice
hut constructed on shore

what remained?   the last struggle
death ever victorious
as one by one the crew
diminished   each laid down
in his turn
in the icy cemetery where I found them

the last   more robust
and more unfortunate than the others

no friendly hand
to tend his last hour
to preserve his remains by pious precautions
became the prey of bears
as soon as he had breathed the last sigh
or even   indeed   so soon
as he could no longer defend himself

31st July 1838

xlvii

blubber — laid upon blocks — hauled up with hand-hooks — chopped — dropped off the block — down into the shallop — removed with a copper ladle — into a great tub — hanging on a gibbet — made to turn — to and again — between blubber board and coppers — emptied — filled — and the shallop — half full of water — cools the oil — cleanses it from soot   and dross — oil runs down a wooden trough — into butts and hogsheads — bunged up — marked and rolled — others set in their place

1614

xlviii

as the bowheads expired
    the lamps ignited
    spreading from the metropolis
    whale-fuelled
    London   Stockholm
    Amsterdam   Lisbon
terraforming
    from darkness
    and the wild
opening up the night
    lighting the way
    for the late-night writer
    for Edward Hopper
    for night trains and day light saving
    CCTV
    24/7 economy
the earth at night
    seen from a satellite
    bright coasts
    rimming
    dark polar holes
places where the Bowheads lived

NOTES

Some passages are translated, edited, added to and rearranged versions of a text by Leonie D'Aunet – the first recorded woman in Svalbard who visited in 1838. She visited at the age of 19 aboard the research vessel, Le Recherche. Her account of the visit appears in *Voyage d'une femme au Spitzberg*.

Passages concerning the process of whaling are similarly arranged segments of the 1613 journal of Robert Fotherby on his first trip to Spitzbergen.

Accounts of Fotherby's 'discovery' of Maudlen Sound are taken from the account of 'The Third Recorded Voyage of William Baffin' recorded by Fotherby. This covers his 1614 voyage.

The final line in part XVI is attributed to Ralph Waldo Emerson.

Parts XXII-XXIV combine texts from tourist guides to Svalbard including: *The Cruise Handbook for Svalbard; Land of the*

Polar Bears — Svalbard Cruise — Albatros Adventure; Cruise Planners – Ocean Princess Sailing on June 6th 2014.

Part XXX is an erasure of *The Treaty between Norway, The United States of America, Denmark, France, Italy, Japan, the Netherlands, Great Britain and Ireland and the British overseas Dominions and Sweden concerning Spitsbergen,* signed in Paris on 9th February 1920.

Part XXXIII is taken from the geographic names website which uses data from American military intelligence: http://www.geographic.org/geographic_names/name.php?uni=-3393177&fid=5888&c=svalbard